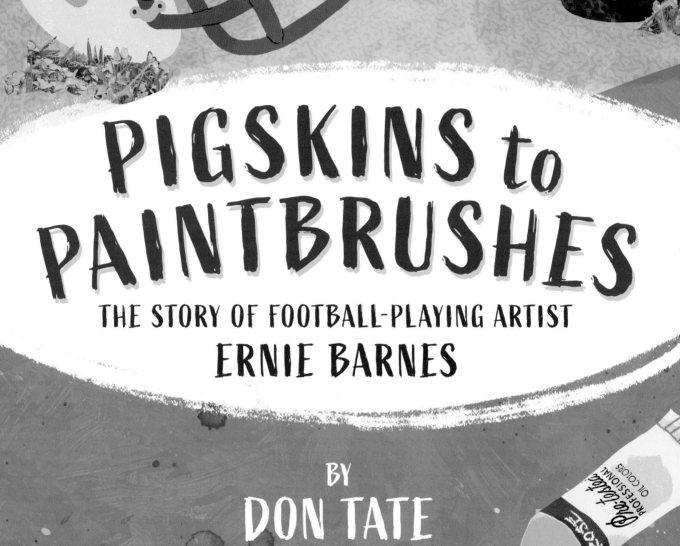

PIGSKINS to PAINTBRUSHES

THE STORY OF FOOTBALL-PLAYING ARTIST
ERNIE BARNES

BY
DON TATE

Abrams Books for Young Readers
New York

The illustrations were rendered with mixed-media collage using Clip Studio Paint and Photoshop.

Cataloging-in-Publication Data has been applied for and may
be obtained from the Library of Congress.

ISBN 978-1-4197-4943-8

Text and illustrations © 2021 Don Tate
Edited by Howard W. Reeves
Book design by Heather Kelly

Printed and bound in China
10 9 8 7 6 5 4 3 2

Abrams Books for Young Readers are available at special discounts when purchased in quantity for premiums
and promotions as well as fundraising or educational use. Special editions can also be created to specification.
For details, contact specialsales@abramsbooks.com or the address below.

ABRAMS The Art of Books
195 Broadway, New York, NY 10007
abramsbooks.com

To my friends at the Highlights Foundation,
where this story first began

Sports didn't come easy for Ernest. He couldn't run very fast. He couldn't dribble a basketball to save his life. No one picked him to play on their teams. Ernest felt pretty lousy about it all. "I couldn't conform easily to the athletic ideal," he once said.

It seemed most everyone expected boys to be good at sports, especially in "the Bottom," a neighborhood of hardworking but poor African Americans in Durham, North Carolina.

Ernest was good at something, however. He was good at art. In his sketch pad, he drew pictures of trees and clouds, animals and people. In the mud after a light rain, he sketched flowing lines all over his yard.

Ernest never said much.
His artwork was his voice.

Opportunities to learn about art were slim for kids in the Bottom during the 1930s. Art museums—as well as restaurants, hotels, and most colleges—were off-limits to Black people. Segregation was the law that kept white and Black people apart.

Laws didn't stop Ernest's mother from finding a way.

Ernest's father was a shipping clerk at a tobacco company in Durham. His mother worked in the home of an attorney—a man who loved classical music and art. Sometimes, she took Ernest along to her job.

While she worked, Ernest scanned art books the attorney had welcomed him to look at, books brimming with the works of revered artists such as Toulouse-Lautrec, Delacroix, and Michelangelo. Bold, expressive brushstrokes. Bright, vivid colors. Long, exaggerated physiques painted Ernest's memories for years to come.

At school, Ernest was a bully magnet. A boy who didn't play sports?
Who loved art, played the trombone, and enjoyed reading poetry? He got
teased for being different. "They hated me," he once said.

One day after class, kids circled around. They shoved Ernest.
They snatched away his trombone. Ernest fell and skinned his knee.

After that, his teachers allowed him to leave school early to avoid more fights. At home, Ernest flooded his sketch pad with hurt feelings. "When I was at home and drawing, I was happy. I made friends with lines," Ernest later said.

The taunts continued in junior high. One day, someone walloped him over the head with a book! Every eye fixed on Ernest. He froze.

"Always drawing," someone said.

"You gonna be an artist, babe?" someone else mocked.

Then someone blurted out, "He ain't got no guts. That's why he won't play."

Play football—that's what real boys do, so many people thought.

When the teasing became unbearable, Ernest dragged himself to the coaches' office and joined the football team.

Practice drills began with an ear-piercing whistle. But Ernest couldn't keep up. Running in a helmet and pads was like exercising in an oven.

The coach fumed. "You never will be nothing!" he yelled. His berating didn't stop there. "You too pretty to play this game!"

That was it. Ernest quit the team.

In high school, the pressure to play football turned up again. *A large boy like Ernest*, everyone thought, *would surely make a great defensive lineman.* Ernest had a plan, though: He instructed his mother to "just say no" should any coaches come snooping around to ask about him joining the team. But she didn't listen.

Over a prayer and a plate of fried chicken, she and the coach made the final decision: Ernest would become number seventy-three on the Hillside Hornets.

Ernest was miserable. But his sketch pad and pencil soothed him. In a quiet hallway far from the football field, Ernest released his troubles onto the page.

Then one day, he got caught.

"What are you doing here, boy?" A voice cut the silence. It was Mr. Tucker, the weight-lifting coach.

He took Ernest's sketch pad.

But then Mr. Tucker smiled. "Did you do these drawings?" he asked.

"Yes, sir," Ernest said.

Mr. Tucker chatted with Ernest about his art. They talked about football and grades, too, and . . . bodybuilding! Turned out, exercise had helped Mr. Tucker to become a better athlete. Could bodybuilding help Ernest to become a better football player?

Maybe. Ernest couldn't wait to find out.

For a while, Ernest's attention turned away from art. Instead, he focused on building muscle. At home, he followed Mr. Tucker's instructions. He exercised and lifted weights. He pushed himself all summer. When football season began in the fall, Ernest was a muscle machine—with confidence to match!

Not only did he play football, but Ernest also became the team captain. Later, he joined the track team, too, becoming state champion in the shot put. By graduation, he had earned twenty-six athletic scholarships to colleges and universities.

After that, no one messed with the six-foot-three, nearly 250-pound lineman again. "I found a groove," Ernest later said. "I loved to win."

No offers came from Duke University, only seven miles from his home—
or from the University of North Carolina. Black players weren't allowed.
Segregation was still the law.

His mom promised him a car if he'd stay at home and attend nearby North
Carolina College—an all-Black school that welcomed him with a full-ride
scholarship. And so that's what Ernest did. He played hard-nosed football.
He heaved the discus and hurled the shot put. But his heart longed to create.

Ernest quit the track team to devote more time to developing as an artist.
"I never left art," Ernest said.

He adored the large studio classrooms, the easels, the sweet smell
of oil paints. He studied anatomy, perspective, light, and shade.
He experimented with new mediums, like charcoal and
inks. And he learned more about art history, too.

Sometimes Ernest got stuck for ideas on what to paint. He asked his art teacher about it. "If you're going to be an artist, you've got to work from your experiences," the teacher told Ernest. "When you're on the field, check out what is going on around you."

Ernest listened. Then he realized how football and art were one and the same. Both required rhythm. Both required technique. Passing, pulling, breaking down the field—that was an art.

For Ernest, art and football could not be divided. From that point forward, he painted images from the game of football.

While Ernest grew up admiring art in books, he'd never actually been to an art museum. Laws prevented that. But now the laws had changed. When an upcoming field trip to the North Carolina Museum of Art was announced, Ernest was over-the-moon excited.

Other than the post office, the museum was the fanciest place he had ever been. Some paintings on the walls were realistic. Others were abstract. Ernest was having a great time, but he also felt disappointed. Something was missing.

"Where are the paintings by Negro artists?" he asked the museum guide.

"I'm afraid your people don't express themselves this way," she said.

Words as cold as ice. Words Ernest knew weren't true.

Laws had changed. People's attitudes had not.

After college, Ernest was ready to pursue a career in art. He even sold his first painting to a basketball player. "The ninety dollars I received was great," Ernest said, "but the real excitement was in having him hang my paintings in his home."

Nothing slowed Ernest's dreams . . .

. . . except for maybe one thing: an offer to play for the American Football League!

On draft day, professional teams chose players, and Ernest hoped to get picked. A career in football could make him a rich man. On the morning of the draft, he opened the sports section of the newspaper and searched for his name. Ernest's hands were sweating; his heart pounded. Several of his teammates were listed, but his name was missing. Then he saw it: "Ernest Barnes, a tackle at North Carolina College."

He dashed out to the garden to show his mom.

"Look, Mama, look! I got drafted by the Colts!"

Wow! Imagine that! The kid from the Bottom, who no one chose to play on their team, was now in demand from the biggest football league in the nation. Ernest would become a professional football player.

The World Champion Baltimore Colts had been eyeing Ernest throughout his college years. Soon, they jetted him off to Baltimore to watch the championship game and to sign a contract.

Ernest could not sleep that night. Excited, he spiraled out of bed and grabbed a paintbrush. Then he expressed his delight on canvas, painting a picture of his new teammates. He named his artwork *The Bench*.

When a sportswriter learned about Ernest, he requested an interview. A football-playing artist? Now there was a story to tell! But when the article was printed in the *Baltimore News-Post*, Ernest's name was misspelled as "Ernie." From that day forward, Ernest Barnes became known as Ernie Barnes. And the football-playing artist was just fine with that.

Officially, Ernie Barnes was a Baltimore Colt. But new players had to make it through training camp before officially making the team, which proved to be tougher than Ernie had imagined. Guys in the big leagues were larger than college players. Muscle-bound bodies bashed. Heads banged. Sometimes clashes were bloody.

Ernie gave his best, but it wasn't good enough. By the final day of camp, he had been cut from the Colts. Ernie was crushed.

He wasn't without a job for very long, though. He was next signed to play for the New York Titans. Later, he played for the San Diego Chargers, before ending up on the Denver Broncos.

Art remained in Ernie's heart, even on the field. Before games, Ernie slipped the stub of a pencil and a notepad into his sock.

During time-outs, he scribbled notes of what he'd seen while playing. He recorded what his body felt like when it moved. He planned how he could splash that movement onto canvas later.

Sketching during team meetings was a big no-no, however. One time, a coach fined him a hundred dollars as punishment. His teammates didn't mind, though—they nicknamed him "Big Rembrandt," after the famous Dutch artist.

Five seasons of football slogged by. Ernie battled on the gridiron, but his heart ached for more time to paint. After an injury, Ernie decided it was time to retire from football. He was twenty-seven years old.

Was his football career over?

Definitely not. Ernie had a plan: At a meeting with league owners, he asked to be hired back. Not as a player, but as an artist—the Official Artist of the American Football League!

The owners got quiet as Ernie pled his case. No one knew quite how to respond. An artist? For a football league? They were confused.

Owners of the New York Jets liked the idea, however, and Ernie soon joined their team—yes, as an artist! He quickly went to work creating thirty new paintings in just a few months.

A solo art show at a Manhattan gallery was soon arranged by Sonny Werblin, the owner of the Jets.

On the night of the exhibition, the gallery quickly swarmed with football players, art critics, sports announcers, and reporters.

Ernie was worried, his nerves like jelly. Had he made a mistake? Would anyone even purchase a painting?

A phone call from his mother calmed him. She offered a prayer, then sent him off to greet his guests.

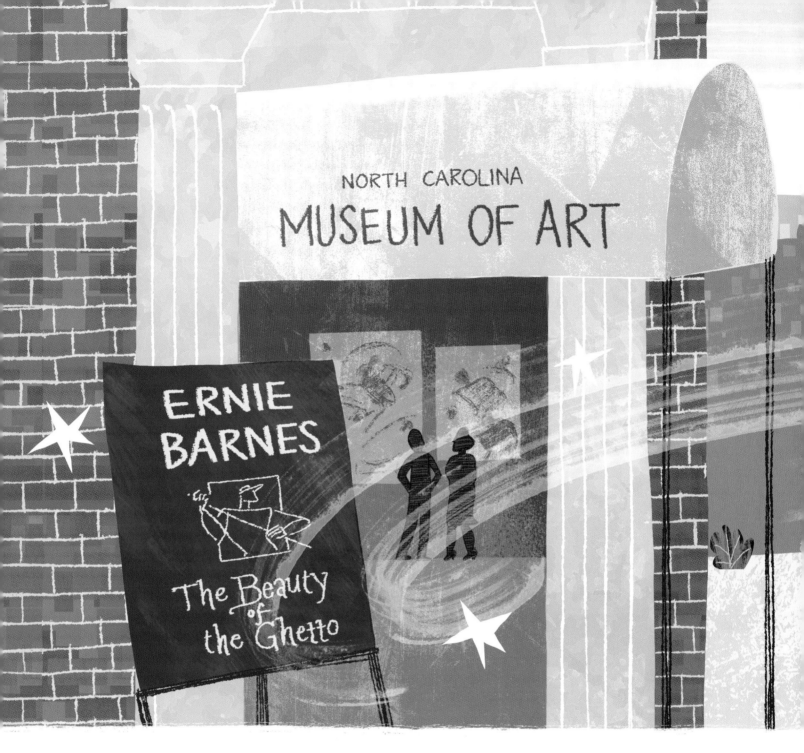

Ernie's paintings were dynamic. Lights and shadows swirled. Lines and patterns sang. The raw muscle of football danced with the grace of a ballerina.

Ernie began painting the people of the Black community he so admired. This collection of paintings he called *The Beauty of the Ghetto*. One of his paintings was featured on the national television show *Good Times*. Ernie even appeared on the show—twice!

In the spring of 1979, Ernie's art career churned full circle, when he exhibited at the North Carolina Museum of Art. Surely he thought about the tour guide from twenty-three years ago, the one who said that Black people didn't express themselves artistically. He must have thought about all the bullies who teased him for wanting to be an artist. Maybe he thought about his father, who had passed away by now and hadn't believed art was a good career choice.

Ernest Barnes had been a boy who liked art. He was shy. He was quiet. Others tried to decide who he should be.

But Ernest decided for himself. He became an athlete. He became an artist. This boy could be anything he wanted to be! "Football demands creativity," Ernie once said.

From pigskins to paintbrushes, Ernie Barnes grew to be a man successful at being himself.

AFTERWORD

Don Tate

During my research, I discovered that there were sometimes conflicting dates about events in Ernie's life. I used *From Pads to Palette*, Ernie's memoir, as my principal source. On a few occasions, I had to make educated guesses based on other events in his life. I am not an official spokesperson for the Ernie Barnes family trust. I am a children's picture book biographer. In my work, I strive to give my readers a taste of a subject's life through words and pictures.

That becomes a challenge in the limited number of pages I have to work with. In addition, telling the story of an iconic and beloved artist, whose works continue to exhibit around the world, presents additional challenges. In telling this story, I was intentional about not creating images representative of Ernie Barnes's artwork, style, or technique. In order to see and enjoy the true artwork of Ernie Barnes in its full glory, please see his official website, ErnieBarnes.com, or other sources listed in the bibliography. (About the title: Early footballs were made of animal bladders—often from pigs. They were inflated and sometimes stuffed with straw or other material. Today's footballs, and those of Ernie Barnes's day, were made of rubber, but the nickname "pigskins" stuck.)

Ernest (Ernie) Eugene Barnes Jr. was a beloved African American artist, football player, actor, and author. He was born on July 15, 1938, in Durham, North Carolina. Barnes's artwork, with its elongated human figures and graceful movement, possessed a similarity of technique and style prevalent during the sixteenth century, prompting an art critic to describe Barnes as the founder of the Neo-Mannerism movement. However it is labeled, Ernie Barnes's artwork is a testament to his love of sports and to the African American experience.

The Barnes family lived on Willard Street, an unpaved road in a poor area of town folks referred to as the Bottom. This was during the Jim Crow era, when Durham was segregated.

Ernie's father, Ernest Eugene Barnes Sr., worked as a shipping clerk for a tobacco company. His mother, Fannie Mae Geer, worked as a domestic. Ernie had an older half brother, Benjamin, and a younger brother, James.

Fannie Mae introduced her children to the arts at an early age, encouraging them to take tap-dance lessons and learn to play several musical instruments. She worked in the home of prominent attorney and school board member Frank L. Fuller Jr., a lover of art and classical music. On the occasions when Ernest accompanied his mom to work, Mr. Fuller shared his art books and discussed his favorite painters with Ernie. Mr. Fuller's discarded classical records and art prints were like gold in the hands of the young artist. By the time Ernest entered first grade, he was familiar with such masters as Toulouse-Lautrec, Delacroix, Rubens, and Michelangelo.

Barnes described himself as overweight, shy, and sensitive, with a mother who dressed him like "the white kids who went to the fashionable private schools." He became the target of bullies throughout his grade school years.

In high school, he turned low self-esteem on its head after a weight-lifting coach taught him about bodybuilding. After that, Barnes became a prolific athlete, earning twenty-six athletic scholarships.

Barnes credits Ed Wilson, the chairman of his college department, with helping him to develop the foundation of his art. Wilson reminded his student that art was all around him and that he should work from his experiences. He advised Barnes to pay special attention to what his body felt like while playing football and then to express that movement in his art.

Ernie Barnes standing alongside one of his paintings at the Grand Central Art Galleries in New York, November 15, 1966. (AP Photo/John Rooney, File)

In 1960, at the dawn of the civil rights movement, Barnes was drafted into the National Football League, an opportunity he could not resist. An art career would have to wait. He played five seasons as an offensive guard. Originally, he was selected to play for the Washington Redskins, who dropped him from the team minutes after discovering he was Black.

By the end of his career, Barnes had grown angry with football—the brutality and violence, the dehumanization of the sport. He retired in 1966 following an injury.

He approached the league owners with the idea of becoming the official artist for the American Football League. The idea lead to his being hired by Sonny Werblin, owner of the New York Jets, "to just paint" for six months, wherein he earned more money than his previous year as a player. A solo art exhibition was then set up, and its success launched Barnes's art career.

As a response to the 1960s Black Is Beautiful movement, Barnes created a series of thirty-five paintings that served as visual love letters to Black America. *The Beauty of the Ghetto* toured major cities from 1972 through 1979.

In most of his later paintings, Barnes portrayed subjects with their eyes closed, a detail that expressed his belief that "most people are blind to one another's humanity, to their inner light." He believed that racism had "taught many of us 'what' to think about each other, but not 'how' to think about one another."

In 1984, Ernest Barnes became the official artist of the Olympic Games in Los Angeles. In 1984, and again in 2004, he was named Sport Artist of the Year by the American Sport Art Museum and Archives. In 1990, Barnes was awarded an honorary doctorate of fine arts by North Carolina Central University.

Barnes won commissions from entertainers of his time—such as Harry Belafonte, Flip Wilson, and Charlton Heston—in addition to more recent celebrities like Kanye West. Barnes's artwork has appeared in magazines and on album covers, while he himself has appeared on television and in movies.

Ernest Barnes died on April 27, 2009.

AUTHOR'S NOTE

As a child, I loved the 1970s television show *Good Times*. It featured a Black family at a time when there weren't many other shows on TV that featured people who looked like me.

One of the main characters was teenage J. J. Evans. He was an artist who painted positive images of Black people with graceful, elongated bodies—his artwork moved. Years later, I learned that J.J. was not the actual artist who created those paintings. The real-life artist was former football player Ernie Barnes. What? I tucked away a mental note until years later, when I'd write this book.

While doing research for this story, I realized that Barnes's childhood experience was similar to my own. I was not good at sports, and I felt inadequate about it. Boys, especially in the Black community where I grew up, were expected to excel at baseball and basketball. But I was always the last choice when teams picked players. I could not dribble a basketball. I could not catch a baseball. While playing right field in Little League baseball, I prayed the ball would not come my way. And football? Just no.

I was an art kid. Researching Barnes's childhood story conjured memories of when I was made to feel less of a boy as I avoided the fast and furious basketball courts during summer camps in favor of coloring or making crafts—most times with a group of girls. Drawing, painting, braiding, sewing, and macramé were some of my favorite pastimes. But these activities ran counter to many others' definition of masculinity.

It wasn't until much later in life that I became drawn to athletics. Not football or basketball—definitely not any contact sports. My sport was bodybuilding. Inspired by my brother, who became an award-winning competitor in natural bodybuilding, I started working out every day. I became a gym rat, loving the gym as much as my art studio. Eventually, I competed in natural bodybuilding, too—and I won!

Today, I am an artist; I draw, paint, and write. Today, I am an athlete, too; I run, swim, and practice yoga daily. And just like Ernest Barnes, I define myself, not letting others decide who I should be.

Front and back of the 1964 Denver Broncos Topps football card. Barnes is shown wearing jersey #55 although his jersey was actually #62. (Topps® trading card used courtesy of The Topps Company, Inc.)

ERNIE BARNES
DENVER BRONCOS   GUARD

48 ERNIE BARNES   guard, Denver Broncos

Height: 6:03   Weight: 243
Age: 25   Years in AFL: 5
College: North Carolina

You might not think that a professional artist would spend his winter months playing football, would you? Well, Ernie Barnes is such a fellow. After graduating from college in '60 with a degree in art, Ernie was signed by the newly formed Los Angeles Chargers in the American Football League. A giant guard, he joined the Broncos before the 1963 season began.

WHICH COLLEGE CLUB IS CALLED "THE QUAKERS"?
PENNSYLVANIA

©T.C.G.   PRINTED IN U.S.A.

NOTES

For more information about the sources below, please see the bibliography.

5   "I couldn't conform . . . athletic ideal": Barnes, *From Pads to Palette*, p. 8.

10   "They hated me": Ibid.

11   "When I was at home . . . I made friends with lines ": Ibid.

12   "Always drawing": Barnes, p. 10.

12   "You gonna be an artist, babe?": Barnes, *From Pads to Palette*, p. 10.

12   "He ain't got . . . won't play": Ibid.

13   "You never will be nothing!": Barnes, p. 11.

13   "You too pretty to play this game!": Ibid.

16   "What . . . here, boy?": Barnes, p. 12.

17   "Did you do these drawings?": Ibid.

19   "I found a groove": Ibid.

20   "I never left art": "Ernie Barnes Links Art and Athletics." *Baytown Sun*, March 13, 1983, p. 11.

22   "If you're going . . . on around you": Barnes, p. 14.

25   "Where are the paintings . . . themselves this way": Barnes, p. 15.

26   "The ninety dollars . . . in his home": Barnes, p. 16.

26   "Look, Mama . . . the Colts!": Barnes, *From Pads to Palette*, p. 17.

38   "Football demands creativity": "Former Pro Gridder Ernie Barnes Sees No Conflict Between Football and Art," *Sioux City Journal* (Associated Press), November 14, 1972; p. 24.

BIBLIOGRAPHY

ARTICLES

Baytown Sun (Baytown, TX). "Ernie Barnes Links Art and Athletics." March 13, 1983.

Clarion-Ledger (Jackson, MS). "Ernie Barnes Paints Portraits in Dignity." September 29, 1974.

Colorado Springs Gazette-Telegraph. "Ernie Barnes Combines Football, Art—Successfully." October 12, 1972.

Daily News (New York). "Beauty in the Ghetto." September 29, 1975.

Durham Sun (Durham, NC). "Barnes' Museum Exhibit Personal Accomplishment." May 17, 1979.

Morning Herald (Durham, NC). "Durham Artist Opens Show." May 20, 1979.

Murphy, Zacki. "Ernie Barnes: Native Son and Artist Extraordinaire." *Herald Sun* (Durham, NC). June 21, 2018. See www.heraldsun.com/opinion/article213558884.html.

Robinson, Louie. "The Violent Brush of Ernie Barnes." *Ebony*, March 1973 (p. 40).

Weber, Bruce. "Ernie Barnes, Artist and Athlete, Dies at 70." *New York Times*, April 30, 2009. See www.nytimes.com/2009/04/30/arts/30barnes.html.

BOOKS

Barnes, Ernie. *From Pads to Palette*. Waco, TX: WRS, 1995.

Hurd, Michael. *Black College Football, 1892–1992: One Hundred Years of History, Education, and Pride*. Marceline, MO: Walsworth, 2000 (p. 63–65).

Wallace, Sandra Neil. *Between the Lines: How Ernie Barnes Went from the Football Field to the Art Gallery*. New York: Simon & Schuster/Paula Wiseman, 2018.

VIDEOS

CNN Tribute to Ernie Barnes (featuring Akili Richards)
  youtube.com/watch?v=T24QlwFuzTo

Ernie Barnes: An American Story
North Carolina Museum of History
  youtube.com/watch?v=7QBj726-bwI

Ernie Barnes Exhibit
North Carolina Museum of History
  www.pbs.org/video/ernie-barnes-exhibit-nc-museum-history-rj7yek

Kareem Abdul-Jabbar for the *Hollywood Reporter*
How Athlete-Artist Ernie Barnes Captured Black Culture's "Joy and Communal Dignity"
  hollywoodreporter.com/news/kareem-abdul-jabbar-how-athlete-artist-ernie
  -barnes-captured-black-cultures-communal-dignity-1209376

WEBSITES

American Sport Art Museum and Archives (ASAMA). "Ernie Barnes, 'America's
  El Greco'—1984 and 2004 ASAMA Sport Artist of the Year." See www.asama.org
  /awards-of-sport/medallion-series/sport-artist-of-the-year/ernie-barnes.

Black Art Depot Today. "Ernie Barnes Biography: From Football Star to Legendary Artist."
  See blackartblog.blackartdepot.com/artist-biography/ernie-barnes-biography.html.

Haley, Alex. "Ernie Barnes / Artist." September 4, 2018. See alexhaley.com/2018/08/11
  /ernie-barnes-artist.

Open Durham. "Ernie Barnes's House." See www.opendurham.org/buildings
  /ernie-barnes-house.

Siegel, Alan. "The Football Journeyman Turned Legendary Artist Who Worked with
  Kanye West and Marvin Gaye." Vice.com, May 21, 2015. See www.vice.com/en_us
  /article/8qpy53/the-football-journeyman-turned-legendary-artist-who-worked-with
  -kanye-west-and-marvin-gaye.

ACKNOWLEDGMENTS

I'd like to acknowledge the following people who played a part in assisting me in some way in telling this story: Emily Grant, Youth and Family Programs Coordinator at the North Carolina Museum of History; Bill Hayes and Carolyn Hayes, who generously offered their time for an interview—Bill was a childhood neighbor of Ernie Barnes; Christopher Ciccone, photographer, North Carolina Museum of Art; the Armadillustrators critique group in Austin, Texas; and Kelly Starling Lyons, Tameka Fryer Brown, and Crystal Allen, colleagues at the Brown Bookshelf website.